# The Night my soul Cried

## by LaRedeaux

# Table of Contents

Spirit..................................................5
Love...................................................17
Reflections.......................................48
Pain..................................................57
Happiness........................................67
Midnight..........................................84
Black................................................91
Move...............................................104

# The Night My Soul Cried

Copyright © 2014 Lashawone (LaRedeaux) Powell

All rights reserved. This work or any portion thereof may not be reproduced, transmitted, stored or used in any form or by any means without prior written consent from the publisher/author. This includes photocopying; record scanning, digitizing, web distribution or information storage and retrieval systems.

The Night My Soul Cried

This is a work of fiction. Names, characters, businesses, places, events and incidents are either the products of the author's imagination or used in a fictitious manner Any resemblance to actual persons, living or dead, or actual events is purely coincidental.

Published by Midnight Publications
Written by: LaRedeaux
Editing: Honorable Menchan Media
ISBN-13: 978-0-9891195-3-5
ISBN-10: 098911953X
LCCN: 2014935528

Printed in U.S.A

∞This book of poetry began as a lump in my throat, extended to the pain in my cries and exited as the tear drops from my eyes. ∞

♥Thank you for your purchase of The Night My Soul Cried. This collection takes me back to my first love, Poetry.♥ XOXO

Pick up other reads by LaRedeaux at
www.midnightpublications.com

# Spirit

*I*nstead of letting go of the hurt and pain we've experienced during our lives, we bury it deep in our hearts. I pushed all the anger, resentment, unforgiveness into the crevice of my soul. Living with poison inside squeezes out the love He has for us unconditionally. The night my soul cried, my Spirit became free.

## Tears of my soul

A tear drops on the palm of my hand,
I'm gripping flowers in the other.
To your grave I come to weep
So we can be close to one another.
Been so hard this thing called life…
How much more can I take?

My heart is weak.
My mind indistinct.
Your guidance is what I seek.
How can I go on without you near?
Your strength…
Your love…
I need you here.

Bowing my head, I began to pray
For only He can take this pain away…
A warm breeze engulfed my soul
Like the way you used to hold…
Your voice resonates in my head,
"Don't cry my dear,
Remember my love, No tears.
I may have left too soon…
Leaving you full of sorrow.
But Heaven required an Angel
To look after you tomorrow.

Today is just a test,
Sometimes, pains brings out the best
Be patient;
Be humble.


Forgive in your heart.
One day we'll know longer be apart.
In your heart, can you understand…
I know longer suffer from man's hands
I'm spending eternity
At beautiful gates of paradise…

## The Greatest gift

His blood did spill so you might live.

It was a gift; His to give

Bow a knee and ask him in

You'll feel Him there just you and Him.

His embrace is like a swarm…

You'll know its existence; lovely and warm.

A change will come slow and sure.

All your sins will vanish for he's the cure

All he requires is for you to believe

Spread the news for all to see.

In doing these simple things.

One day you'll behold the King

## Always the same

Come and rest you head here
Let me wipe away your tears
The world is hard and so unkind
But you can make it rewind
Watch the replay
Learn from the mistakes
You're tired that's okay
Let's sit down and pray
God gives us strength
He gives us power
Increasing with every passing hour
Look to Him then you will see
Only then you're set free
I have had my share of the heartache and pain
And sometimes my faith begins to wane
I have no money or no fame
When no one's there He remains the same
Just behold His powerful name

## Breaks

Many thanks to God for the guidance
                        Those little whispers into my soul.
For making me to break
                        Only to return renewed and whole.
Many thanks to God for humanity
                        For reality... the puzzle that it is!
All the comedy & tragedy
                        The sorrow and the bliss.
Many thanks to God for the family,
                        Who will forever be as one…?
No matter who is here or there?
                        Nor what remains or is gone.
Many thanks to God for the music and lyrical treats
                        That got me through
The beat of the heart
                        That dances is me and you.
Many thanks to God for the awakening
                        Many thanks to God for the dream
That paved every step in-between.
                        Thank you for the pen
That could be a feather or a knife
                        For it holds the power of Death and Life!

## Fear

The Truth of the matter is...

*I'm scared!*

Though, I'm not afraid...I know fear

It's right here...I'm vulnerable & terrified

*I swear!*

Encourage, and proclaim...

With unusual exhilaration

Fortified!

By the tenets, of my Lord's Prayer,

I dare...To strive for enlightenment

...Out in the open...

Struggling, but coping, with foreboding lies

Trying to surmise, what's the world deems "FAIR"

Trusting, it's sufficient...Hoping, God will still care

Comfort me in my despair

And grant me the courage, to bear…

To carry, whatever ridiculous notions,

I may not quite comprehend

Until that time I fully understand,

the Almighty's encompassing glory

*Love's* all-inclusive plan

Regardless of the accusatory sins,

that deem me unworthy

I take my stance **BOLDLY!**

# Fear

((Secure))

Already knowing,

my soul is ongoing and my place is assured

Throughout Eternity...

Holy...Within

Something akin, to Peace everlasting

True Joy...with...The One

...**Omega**~

Beginning and End...

## I apologize

I didn't mean for my
Veins to drip on the page
With my red slick fingers
These words
Triggered me to jump out
The glass window of my sight
Wander in the night
Drunken on air
Hungry for grace and mercy
Crawling
Back before dawn
Broken but alive
To scribble
Bloody thanks
For the slap in the face
To wake up
And live
For I've got so much more to give

## Four little letters

Four letter word troubling me for a purpose
Offered the dictionary, I can't seem to define it.
It doesn't make sense when I think about it
And come up with a purpose for it
It is a beautiful thing, Fascinating to say the least
But without a purpose, feels like a burden uncouth
I haven't done the things I should have done
For God's sake I'm knocking on 41
Worn out for a purpose I won't simply find.
Hoping that time will tell, my true purpose in life
I thank God for blessing me, He paid the price.

## The Night My Soul Cried
### Help me please...

I need some sympathy,

To get through another day,

Help me...please

Weary of this anguish,

It won't go away,

Please won't you help me?

I need just a bit of confidence

I'm always down in the dumps

I need some inspiration

To end the cycle of repeating everything

I need some hope

I feel like I'm always failing… failing (just a thought)

I need some faith

I believe I have lost my own.

Help me…please

Is my cry

Help me…*please*

Before I die

On bended knee's he heard your cry

No longer falling and Lost

He paid the ultimate cost.

## Love is the mirror

*Love* is the mirror  
Through which I see  
The inspirational  
Portion of *me*  
The veil is lifted  
The light within  
Shines through my eyes  
Yet **sees** no sin  

Fear lurks in the *mirror*  
Through which I can know  
The part of **myself**  
That I hid, so long ago  
Within lies the truth  
Of who I really am  
When I listen **faithfully**  
I hear it once again  
It was only a delusion  
A fragment well played  
It is time to transcend  
And see what we made  
Not **righteous**, not **depraved**  
**No judgments to convey**  
No guilt to bestow  
Only love to awake  
When we focus our love  
With an open awareness  

We unite our *soul*  
With the *Divine*

# Love

*L ove is a verb.*
*From the moment we are born until the day we die, we should love others as we love God or ourselves. When love is unconditional it gives without cost or celebration.*

*Love is gentle*
*Love is kind*
*Love doesn't hurt and*
*Yes Love can heal.*

*The night my soul cried, I remembered to Love* **ME!**

*LaRedeaux*

## *Drift away*

You wrapped your lips around mine,
and breathed in deep,
Air from my lungs as I felt you creep.

Under my feet and carry me away,
Beyond the shore, and into the bay.
Petrified and stoned, my pulse on pause,

I almost couldn't feel the cut from your claws.
A swift slice beneath my breast,
and plunged wrist deep:

Where my heart had rest, my eyes, they peaked.
Your hair was down, a wave of autumn leaves,
Determination in your eyes,
a rush as your grip squeezed.

Twist and a jerk, my body released,
Blood drained through your fingers
as my life begun to cease.

Mixing into the salt and framing the scene,
My blood glistened from your eyes

and I began to dream.

I saw us, I felt us,
walking hand in hand,
I felt the first day of our wedding bands.

Late nights, summer, winter, and the future,
I saved all as gifts that life let us nurture.
Just before it all faded away,

I felt the words of the last kiss you made.
You released my body limp
into the sea and trailed toward the land,
My heart drained of life, yet the love remained in your hand

*Drift away*

## We are one

You make me *smile*.
You make me *laugh*.
You make my heart beat 100 times too fast.
My knees go *weak*.
My heart skips a *beat*.
My body gets *aroused* when you're near me.
My mind draws a *blank*.
Our love grows *strong*.
You make feel like I'm the only one.
Like it's just *you and I*.
You gave me your *heart*.
As I gave you *mine*.
We're two bodies, yet intertwined
Our love soars high like birds in the sky.
You without Me I could surely die

**I LOVE YOU, MY LOVE**

## Before I knew you...

I loved you...before I ever knew you.
Please understand this love started long
before physicality came into play.

It stemmed from the bareness of your soul,
Not your bare body.
I fell in love with your naked mind,

Not your beautiful naked body.
It wasn't that sexy seductive look in
your eyes that seized my attention,

But the vulnerability and anguish you still carried.
I wanted to know what it was like to be with you,
By that I meant in your mind,

What are your fears?
Your hopes?
What are your dreams?
What things have you seen?

What are the experiences that merged together and
Created the beautiful soul standing in front of me?

## Before I knew you...

Who was responsible for your broken
heart and your inability to trust?
What mistakes make you believe
you are good enough to be loved?

Or that you don't deserve to be loved?
I sought to be inside your mind,
I desired to be in the darkest parts of your heart,
I needed to be there from the start,

From the day you put yourself back
together from all the pain.
I sought the day you decided to remove the shackles,
taking away your freedom…,

The freedom to love wholeheartedly,
To give your all,
The day you demolished fear,
The disease, spreading from your heart to your mind.

I needed to be here the day you finally
let someone else in,

## Before I knew you...

And I wanted that person to be me.
My love don't you see?

I loved you before we ever touched,
I fell in love with the person I knew that you could be,
The person standing in front of me today….
The one who today fully knows their worth,
The one who despite the fear no longer
lets it control them.

With hope and faith I'll never hurt you,
Our love and bond will last,
*I loved you before I ever knew you*

## *Love and Peace*

I could never face it,

I kept running

Running…

Only to realize there's no end to this road,

I kept telling myself not to think

Not to feel

Just to be.

But truth is, I'm tired

*Love…*

You're no good for me

Yet I crave you

Why is that?

I poured my heart out to you

Time and time again

To love you so selflessly,

Only for a little while

Now, I can't remember

How it once felt

When I just wanted to hear your voice

To feel the things I once caressed

While you were vital to me.

## Love and Peace

My beloved, you walked all over me
Here I am crawling behind you.
A *Queen*, who lost sight of her royalty
Trying please a man she once saw as *King*

But I've learned,
Love wouldn't do those things to me
And no matter how much it hurts,
I'm much better without you,
My love will never cease
For I have found peace

## That thing you do

You know that thing you do
When you do that,
I'm enslaved to the essences of you,
And you...
The many color's upon my wings
On the breeze,
Painting your strokes over my canvas,
Your embracing kiss,
Dripping your in unto me.
You know that thing you do…
When you do that,
I'm lost in you
Revealing
Surrendering
To your soft cuddling,
Your shades displaying my love,
With each stroke
That thing you do…
Leaves me falling for you

## In the End...

I forgot the feeling of a lover's real kiss
I forgot the main reason, the point to all of this
I forgot why I even want this so bad
I forgot and I don't know why I'm feeling so mad
Tears fall and I don't know the reason why
Folks always leave the beast and make her cry
I'm patiently waiting for him to have a reason to leave
For my issues to become one of your pet peeves
I know you love me but really, for how long?
And I know you belong with me but
my faith isn't very strong?
Why do I torment myself seeking this life?
Ripping shards of my heart, cutting like a knife
Then I remember that *Love's* worth the pain
You can't have a rainbow
without a little *Rain*

## Hopelessly Renewed

Laying on my floor, room still a mess,
You on my mind, weighing heavy on my chest,
Memories flood my mind, of all our amazing times,
Love and pain flood my heart, it's a good sign,
Once, unable and unwilling to feel,
Fear chasing away happiness,
Now I'm in love, filled with distress,
You opened my heart, warmed my frozen soul,
Wanting me to love you, my heart your goal,
Eagerly I gave in, needing to feel alive,
Forever seeking happiness, to help me survive,
I hate being alone, used and full of distrust,
Throwing up walls, through them you bust,
Suddenly exposed, I cling to you in hope and fear,
Holding you close, I'll keep you forever near,

My love,
My heart,
My soul,
no one can take me from you,
For with you, my love is strong...
And renewed.

## Friends with Benefits

I think we should just be friends.

                I can't lose you over some bullshit.
I couldn't stand to part from you due to small petty

        Arguments and small insecurities we are all guilty of.
You're much more to me than that.

              I adore you and want to hold you close.
We can still share a mattress.

                We can still build fortress,

Out of sheets

        Hide away from the sun till our realities tear us apart.
But I do want to be intimate with you on higher levels

        I want to dive into you and inspect every aspect
…of your fast paced thought process.

              I want more than to exchange gifts
…on seemingly pointless, media endorsed holidays.

                I want to exchange ideas.

Expand my mind instead of just

        the space between my thighs.
We can still fight like an ordinary couple

        if that offers any consolation.

# ...Friends with Benefits

We can argue till all we can do is stare at each other
                         Mentally begin to undress one another.

The fire we both inherited
            Can keep us warm during cold nights.
And we can cling desperately to each other's limbs
            Like well never see each other again.

And we can ramble on about things
                         we won't remember in the morning.
We can laugh at stupid shit and not once stifle
                Our true selves in an attempt
                    to come off as attractive.
Let our intellect allure one another.
                      I am already smitten with your personality.
Your grace, humor and sensibility
                        So I've been in it for the long run.
I'm saving you for every rainy day to come.
                                A secret pleasure.

## My Friend.....with Benefits

## Soul Maybe?

Is there such a thing as a soul mate?
Or a soul maybe?
Just a state of mind
Deep connection, unity, great fits,
Love that's absolutely real
The idea that two people that are
"meant to be together" is false
Love can incubate anywhere
"*Soul mate*" a nice thought,
but soul maybe
Until you find out he has another babe…
Is there such a thing as "soul mates"
Or just fortunate and unfortunate events,
People who are in love

# I ____ U!

Why do we say it?
Loosely with our lips

Those three little
Lightening words?

Why does it stand strongly?
For so much

When it can easily fall
Apart for so little?

Why does it have such power?
Over our hefty hearts

When we need strength
To keep it beating?

Why do the eyes tell?
The open mind

That the flesh is

*I \_\_\_\_\_ U!*

...for the taking?

Why do we crown
...beauty with gold

Every time we wish
...to claim it as our own?

Why keep asking
Question after question

We don't know any other way
So we utter the words you long to say...

*I \_\_\_\_\_ U!*

# *Irreconcilable*

"……I'm going back to a place that's far away
How 'bout you? I know you've got a place to stay
Why should I care, when I'm just trying to get along?
We were friends but now it's the end of our love song…"

If my lips could touch your face
Gently kiss all the hurt away
Then it would have already been done
I'd have done it right now….. Today

Love professed so strongly by two
Quickly melts into a lonely sea of one
The pain of the severed member
Affects the very existence of the other one…

Halves no longer whole and pain is no longer new,
The damage of a perfect love so real
Seemingly can't be undone
We're worlds apart, baby what can we do?

Our time becomes lost in the cacophony of
Anger, rage, disdain and distrust.
Troubled waters disintegrate a beautiful masterpiece
It becomes but a white noise,
A cantankerous bucket of rust
That blows away and eventually lost….
….never again found

Where has our love gone?
 Why do we fight so hard to be so damned strong?
…..winning the battle but losing the whole damned war
The strength of our love was always the power of two
But you have closed dark shades upon my bright light

I'm growing weary of the anguish
My soul knows not what to do......
....you have from the beginning been
so much more than a crush or muse.

You became my life.
If a tender kiss on your eyelid
Could wash the pain away,
I'd be there right now, I'd be there today

Yet in this repugnant minute of our picturesque now,
I'm having trouble finding a way
I'm quite lost....

....I feel this time my forever is truly gone.
...so let's leave it alone
Seems we can't see eye to eye

There is no good guy
There is no bad guy
There's only you and me
We just disagree...

## Two chords of one note

We are very much the same…You and I
Finding completion through the other
Everything else is just a distraction
The veil of otherness presuming to hide from us
This truth is what I hear in my heart
The strong feelings that just won't go away
The way I feel when your eyes dance
The way I feel when we talk or make love
The way I feel when you read my poetry
Admiring my artful words
The way you are uniquely you
And fit me like a puzzle piece without glue
Everything else is just a distraction
From this truth

## Our Big Day...

Did it just get colder?
I don't feel it when you hold me tight.
I just want to lay my head on your shoulder.
Stay with me and keep me warm tonight.

I'm no longer so shy,
I've gotten much bolder.
When I'm with you I fly.
You don't need to let your feelings smolder.

When I'm with you there's no need to cry.
I know you tremble with fright.
You know you never need to lie.
The feeling like you need to fight,

You can let it out with one big sigh.
Let me quell your appetite.
Let all the unhappiness die.
I'll hold you a while,

Forever if need be
I'll never put you on trial.
You'll always have me.
I just want to be your oasis,
Your little foreign fantasy.

I want to freeze us in stasis,

## Our Big Day...

I can be with you forever.
You are my shining knight.
Your compliments are always so clever,

Really it's alright,
You don't have to tell me how you feel.
I see it all in your eyes.
I'd be happy to reignite a strong seal,

Not one that you can just buy.
My face burns bright,
My room you cannot enter,
It's bad luck to be in your sight.

I'm happy like I've never been.
My dress is so very white.
When the man stops talking… you'll kiss me then,
I shush, then kiss.
So happy to spend my life,
I'll just smile 'cause I'm your wife.

# Honeymoon's Over

I'm half in love

Half in hate

It's like my left

Hand is pushing…you away

My right hand…pulling you in.

My bones are

Aching for your

Touch, but

My lips

Are screaming

…for you to leave.

A civil war

Within my body

…at one in the morning.

I'm terrified…to find out

…who wins…

## Love's Drug

I remember when our love was like a drug.
Our eyes met for the first time and,
You were so righteous and divine,
Smiles and sunshine swept across our faces.
Our love drug took us so many places.
Filled with a high, sweet like cocaine's nectar.
Making love under the stars,
Enticed by the sight of the moonlight.
Lit up by the dark night skies.
Bewildered and burning passion
running through me
Our blood boiling with our love drug.
For many days and nights.
Carrying us throughout the
summer and seasons past.
Our love strong and vast.
I wanted it to last forever.
I remember when our kindred spirits met.
I remember when I knew you were my soul mate.
The words you said the way you held me close,
telling me you are mine.
You were kind and always by my side.
I remember when our love was our drug.
Sweet like cocaine's nectar.
I wanted it to last forever.....

## We shared a moment in time...

There's nobody left to blame
We just ran out of feeling
The impossible became possible
Tears have all dried
You were my desire plateau
My hummingbird in flight
It came out of nowhere
We crashed and burned
Let's celebrate the highs
There's too many to count
Beautiful love affair
Our moment in time…

## Move on...

Still holding on to me
Even after all these years.
Lashing out at me with words
That's wrapped in all your fears.

Telling me it's not your fault,
You don't know what to do.
Yet you'd rather believe the worst,
Even if it's not true!

You get your information
From wherever you can.
From junkies, whores and liars,
You just don't give a damn.

Taking it as gospel,
I fight a rising tide.
Of bullshit propaganda,
That takes you for a ride.

Posted up on Facebook,
With no thought to anyone else.
Cause that's your only comfort,

## Move on...

Who cares what I felt?

Your empty apologies
Constantly ringing through the phone.
It's no wonder you're stuck there,
In newly wed house, feeling so alone.

I don't know what you want,
But please just let me be.
I can't stand your obsessing
You're no longer the second half of me.

## Too little, too late

There was a time you were truly the one.
Now those days are done.
I gave all of who I am to please you,
My love you seemed to misconstrue.
Now you've decided that I'm worthwhile,
You love the fact I'm always able to make you smile.
I understand how I make you feel,
The reasons you stick around.
The love I used to have for you was indeed profound.
But the hurt you dealt me was so real,
You wanted Amy, Tracy or was it Janelle…
My mind, remembered that one time…
Before just the thought of you made me ecstatic,
Now even your sweet nothings seem so anticlimactic.
I did love you, I swear I did.
Oh the ways I loved you,
but the many infidelities you hid.
My trust and love I cannot knowingly misplace.
Because you see in my heart you've created this null space.
Admittedly you still possess the power
to make my heart soar,
But at the end of the day, my heart is always sore

## Fixation

He stood before me with blood shot eyes…
As he held the gun…
And I held the knife…
Broke my heart it did…
For the one l once love is before me

He's the one who wants to take my life
"If I can't have you, no one will"
Through murderous determined eyes
There's no escape I know
Tonight I'll probably die

My body joins my spirit already in the sky
We had such a perfect life
He was my armor, he was the light
Until he got dark,
Until he became the night

Possession and obsession became his desire
So I made a choice and took flight
It angered my once love
One night he sent a letter,

"No matter what, you'll always be mine,"

For a while I was free

Going on with my life

## ...Fixation

Till one night I came home
To meet the man I hadn't seen in a while
So here I stand
In my small kitchen

Trembling with the metal blade in my hand
Sharp breaths and pleading eyes
"Don't," I barely cried…
"Why did you go?"

His tone as cold as ice..
"I loved you so much,"
"Now you must die,"
I closed my eyes in anticipation of the imminent end

But…….nothing happened
My eyes opened again…
He was still standing at my fore
The gun wasn't pointed at me no more

But now at my once lover's head
"I can't, I love you too much,"
With trembling lips I choose this instead,
I was too perplexed to register what he meant

In a flash and click
My deranged lover……ended it…

*The Night My Soul Cried*

# Beautiful Flames

The beautifully wicked flame

It draws me in,

So magnetic,

The closer I get

The hotter it is,

Wanting to feel the beauty

To touch it

To be one with it,

All the while knowing

Burning intense

Pain will follow

And perhaps a tear,

But I do it anyway

Letting it singe my skin

Making what was once so pretty

Into an ugly hurtful monster,

I pull back

Hand still ablaze,

Looking back into that

Beautiful fucking flame

# Reflections

*If you see something on television that you don't like, you change the channel. But what happens when you look in the mirror. Often times we see things in our own reflection that we don't like, yet we do nothing about it. Change is not an easy task. Removing all the hurt, anger, resentment and emotions that have built up from years of abuse requires an active participant. YOU!*

*The night my soul cried, I looked in the mirror and saw the reflection of a distraught soul.*

## In the mirror

Tears flow from my eyes
Like a river overrun after a rainfall
My mind floating away
With no end in sight
A river never really ends
It flourishes with each drip released into it
And narrows with each ray of sunshine absorbing it
Even when the last drip is absorbed
There is still a path left in the earth
Reminding the sun that there is nothing left to take
And leaving the rain with nowhere to thrive

## Life's Book

I want to slip between the pages of life's book,
Encase myself in its words and pages
Sinking slowly through the depth
of language and understanding

I want to become part of the flowing sentences of
fate it may reveal,
I want to discover and experience
Destinies fashioned among the subtle
Intricate paragraphs of existence.

I want to lose myself in the epitaphs of others,
To share the celebrations of their lives
and the longing memories death creates.

I want to be a part of the great epitome
And epiphany of thoughts and explanations
Finding places where whole chapters of verse,
love and life originate.

I want to scribble something across the flyleaf
To serve as a reminder I was there at all,
I want to experience my own sense of reality
I want to be found among those scriptures.

## ...Life's Book

I want to find the memories of that minuscule
Moment in time I was given the chance to fill.
I want to be a part of its past, present and its future
A memory within it.

>Deep within those letters,
>
>Words,
>
>Sentences,
>
>Paragraphs and chapters,
>
>Among the majors and minors,
>
>The loves,
>
>The victories,
>
>The triumphs,
>
>The failures,
>
>The lost and the lonely

I want; somewhere in that huge
databank of complete existence
To be found and wondered about,
For a tiny miniscule moment in time.
I just want to be *remembered*..

## Pretty Girl Blues

The words flow with the tears,
Damp like the rain.
I must be gorgeous,
If beauty is pain...
Your words, they hurt;
Not as much as mine.
A walking travesty,
Yet you call me a dime.
Evil and twisted,
Vile deep inside.
So very much to say,
In whom can I confide?
Fight back the tears,
Hidden behind lies.
Emotionless I seem,
Nowhere left to hide.
Feeling breathless again?
Living life with no air...
Please don't put me on a pedestal,
None can compare.
I am heartless, I am evil.
I am sorry, it is true.
All I can hope,

Is not to destroy you.
I'm fragile and dependent,
Very easy to break.
So listen to these words,
Make no mistake.
Don't call me beautiful,
You haven't seen the scars:
Don't tell me I'll be okay,
I barely got this far.
Made with layers,
Appearing to be sane.
But inside of my head,
Darkness calls my name.
A simple little girl,
Left dejected too many times.
My only way to speak,
These words put into rhyme.
Quiet as a mouse,
Yet slick as fox.
Been pummeled too many times,
Like a stack of wooden blocks.
I rise up again broken,
Injured… beyond repair.
What I've learned is when you're down,
Nobody is there…

## Window to the Soul

Feelings are overrated emotion
Emotions are raw feelings not devotion
Love can warm your heart or make it bleed
It can stand strong or bring you to your knees
With no emotion and nothing to feel
Can't decipher, don't know fantasy from real
Which is better, which is worse?
Are they a blessing or a curse?
They falter anyway the wind blows
There is only one way to know
Look in the eyes
The window to the soul

## Reflections

I look in the mirror

What do I see?

Me looking at you

You glaring at me

I hate eyeing at you

You hate beholding at me

However I'm still looking at you

You're still looking at me

Around and around

Life's like a merry go round

'Till I stop looking at you

And start beholding me

*La Redeaux*

## Abandoned...

Why do the words elude me today?
Usually I can't keep them in
They need to be written
Need to be shared
Heard
Repeated
Felt on the tips of tongues
Chewed on and digested
Given to someone else
They want to run wild on the hearts of youth
Kiss their secret lover's lips
Swaddle an infant in their arms
But today they shy away
I have nothing to say
Nothing's real
Nothing to make you feel
Why has my gift abandoned me today?

# Pain

Pain comes from many sources. It hurts a lot when an enemy hurts you. It hurts more when a friend hurts you, but it hurts the most when the person you love hurts you.

The night my soul cried, I realized know matter how deep you bury the pain, like hot air, it will rise.

## Inside of Me

The pain lives inside of me

Pain of regret,

Pain I can never forget

Pain of memories of a time we once shared

Thinking and wondering if you ever really cared

Pain lives inside of me

Pain of shame

The pain of letting my heart free again

Pain of wanting to love

This pain won't let me be

All I can feel is this pain inside of me

## Pain... What is pain?

Pain what is pain
Different types of pain none all the same
Pain is when you're a child full of shame
Reprehensible things no child should feel
Some kinds of pain that will never heal.
When a child should be out in play
Yet it keeps her locked away
Inappropriate touches to a child
Death would be mild
Screams of echoing pain
Deafening, and inhumane
Like pushing an eggplant through a pin hole
Purity and innocence being stole
Time drudges on for an eternity
Begging and pleading to God "Amen"
The pain of an inappropriate touch
No one to turn to, No one to trust
The tears roll down her face
Her last bellow of disgrace.
Even as an adult there is no escape
The pain of a child being raped
That's what pain is!

## My Pain

My pain was nothing,

It wasn't even there,

My pain never existed,

It lingers without care

My pain is caused by you,

This weakness leaves me blue.

My pain comes from years of abuse,

Never leaving me with a dry eye

My pain won't leave me alone

It hinders relations with friends.

My pain caused many scars.

It is my biggest weakness

My pain means nothing to anyone else

It's driven me into bleakness

## Snow

I will soothe your **pain**
I will make it all okay.
I will make you **happy.**
That's what SNOW told them to say
I will fuck up your **life**
I will **ruin** you
I will make you **suffer**
Is what SNOW brought to my life everyday…
Sure, it numbed the **pain.**
But in the end, it was still there.
Was SNOW the cure?
How much pain should one endure?
The pain of being abused,
Abandoned…
Raped…
And alone…
I thought snow was my **cure,**
But all it did was drown me in the **sewer…**

## Sweet Pain

I leave there sweating
And in pain
The taste is sweeter than anything
Am I twisted and in love with pain?
I feel more alive
The closer I get to demise,
Yet to climax now would be too soon.
I focus on the pain it's the only
Thing that's real.
Pain is weakness leavening the body.
I find myself growing
Increasingly alive, full of life.
I constantly test myself,
Pushing to new heights.
There is a beast within racing for
Unquenchable thirst for victory

## There's levels to this...

Pain at a level of one
It's mild and almost none
Some pain levels can match
A splinter and a scratch
A fall or a broken bone
Can make you bellow or moan
If you gain some weight
That can be a painful state
Even at the level of a ten
Pain fluctuates between women and men
The expiration of a love has tears
That's the worst and can last many years

## Jump Start

My heart I give to you
…only you
Stitched and sealed
So i wont feel…
The pain of yearning each day
Smashed and broken
Bloodied and soakin'
Two bolts
One on each side
Go on give it a jump start
My heart I give to you
So treat it well
Or just go to hell

## Bunions

I feel the pain searing through my veins,
Leaving my toe going,
Straight to my head,
It relit the fire sheltered away in my heart,
Now I'm fuming!

Oh yes I'm seething!

Yet again I'm enraged!

An invisible smoke blowing out my ears,
My teeth gritted,
My body shudders.
My fingers twitch,
And my eyes are crossed.
"Murder" is carved in red
…on my forehead.
The nerve or her….!
HOW DARE SHE…!!!?
..Ignite my pain and walk away!?

## Numb

Someone help
I'm brain dead
My soul's lying wide awake
In a body death forgot to take
My stomach is a Bitch
Can't get you off my mind
All this pain I keep
Please lord, grant me sleep
I'm stuck here alone
Trapped inside my head
Screaming voices in my ears
Blind without sight to see
The shadows still haunt me
Place to place I go
Just ceaselessly and half asleep
Nightmares engraved behind my eyes
Gouge them out leave me dead....

# After the pain Happines reigns...

After the pain, you can be happy again. If you want to feel and be peaceful and happy, start by identifying what that looks like—what you think about, what you feel, what you do, how you interact with people. The night my soul cried I remebered there is Happiness after the pain.

*LaRedeaux*
*Ever After*

Learning to be happy
Is one of the hardest things?
I look at you
I'm jealous when I should be happy.
You're happy and going to have
an amazing life together,
I'm trying to be happy for you.

## Happiness

A joy,
A wonder,
A treasure,
To share
With others...
Happiness
A flower
Which blooms...
When spread
Throughout the world...
Happiness
A feeling
An emotion,
Gratification
When something nice
Is done
For you.

*LaRedeaux*

## *Happiness in...*

Happiness in sunshine,
Happiness in rain.
Happiness in happiness,
Happiness in pain.

Can be found between
Such is time again
Happiness is seen
It can't be feigned.

Happiness in four walls
Open window panes,
Happiness is madness
Let loose, thoughts contained.

Happiness for someone
Puts loneliness to shame
Happiness in everything,
Is happiness' game.

Happiness is a stranger,
For those left in chains
Happiness the reason
Is all left to gain?
Happiness will make you

The child there within,
Happiness will take you
Away from your sin.
Happiness will cultivate you

A garden within
Where wild bees and flowers
And butterflies can swim.
Happiness will reap your
Harvest like a billhook,
Yet Sometime I feel
That happiness
Is nothing more
Than a myth..

## Where it resides

Happiness resides
In this plastic,
On the other side
Of these keystroked verse.

Happiness resides
On this white screen
The clacking sound
Black script...serene.
Happiness resides
In this dull glow,
Electronic pulsations
Conveying my thoughts from
me to you.

## Striving

Is happiness far out of reach?
Something for which we must strive.
Like some far off destination,
Where we hope someday to arrive.
Or is happiness just a commodity?
Something that can be bought,
Or is happiness something we all can learn?
Something that must be taught.

Is our happiness in short supply?
That may someday come to an end,
Or is there enough to go around?
That we can share it with a friend.
There are many things we'll never know,
Like an envelope that's always sealed,
And yet as we pass through life,
The answers are slowly revealed.

For we are all here for a reason,
As we pass from young to old,

## Striving

And the longer that we live it,
The more answers will unfold.

And though we entered the world that way,
We were never meant to be alone,
And though we may often try,
We can't do it all on our own.
For I believe happiness is our purpose,
And a purpose made to share,

To help make happy the ones we love,
And show them that we care.
And whatever our purpose in life may be,
And only time will truly tell,
My only hope is that I've served it,
Served my purpose well.

## Blind Happiness

You told me you LOVE me
Made me believe it
Showed me you didn't
I couldn't conceive it
Waiting and waiting
For you again
Come on tomorrow
New life must begin
Over, over AND over again
Digging out this hole
One thing I've learned
Happiness comes from the soul
Happiness I pursue
Peace I will find
Hopefully soon
Before I lose my mind

*LaRedeaux*

## Felicitations

You are now happy
I am glad for you
Here is a warning
Enjoy it
Savor every moment
Don't let it wound you
Don't leave yourself open
It will consume you
It will change
It can turn pure joy;
Into nothing but pain
It can turn you
Into something you're not
It has its traps
Don't get caught
I don't mean to scare you
I am just giving you some advice
Happiness is amazing
Yet even bliss has a price

## For a moment

If just for a moment,
I got to see his face,
I would be happy
For a moment,

I got to look into his eyes
Feel that love again,
I would be happy

If just for a moment,
I got to feel his lips,
Gently embracing against mine,
I would be happy

If just for a moment,
I got to hear his sonorous voice
That always made smile,
I would be happy

If just for a moment,
To smell his unique, intoxicating scent,

## ...For a moment

I would be happy
If just for a trice
I could feel his strong arms
Embrace me

Innocent love in the world,
I would, be truly happy.
If I just had a moment.

# At Last

A very happy day,
Was the day I met you.
I didn't know what to say,
Wasn't sure what to do.

My heart is beating fast,
And I feel so strange inside.
You remembered me at last,
And you're always at my side.

Following the stars light,
Down a path of broken hearts...
You slowly entered my sight,
My life could truly start.

Such a happy moment,
When you took me in your arms.
I will always treasure it,
I will keep the memory from harm.

*LaRedeaux*

## ...At Last

So this poem is for you,
From a girl whose fallen so completely.
Something you already knew,
But I still hope you'll always be with me.
I love you so much, that is obviously true.

You're the best person that's come to hold my hand.
If you were to let go I'm not sure what I'd do,
I'd be so helpless without your love that I understand.
In this special time of year.
There isn't much else I can say,
But I'm happy as long as you're near...
At Last

## I am Happy

The black ashes are removed,
The paths are conked out,
The meadows haunted with breathing air,
The nature is smiling tearfully,

I am happy.
The light disperses flawlessly,
The spectrum glows conspicuously,
The bees and butterflies sucking the love,
The pleasure is summoning from the distant field,

I am happy.
The rain gets accolades for its true dance,
The sun glows with habitual delight,
The trees are showering its blessings,
The lucid water is fluttering,

I am happy.
The graceful moon is cheering,
The silent night is whispering,
The secrets are revealing,
The stars are winking....at me.
And I am happy

## From the brink...

I'm so happy
So very happy
When I talk to you
Or see your smiling face
I try to hide the dark in me
That is hard to explain
A part of me unwelcome
...or desired
I try to show what's inside
On my mind but it's hard
I close my eyes and think
It's really tough
I think of you and smile
Thoughts of them make me cry
No understanding why
Why i suffer the way i do
You open my eyes anew
I see more than you think
You brought me out of the brink

## New Day

My darkest days are over
My heart no longer a prisoner...
Freed by an exorcism within
Sun warms my skin
Soft songs caress my lips
Laughter tickles the air
that surrounds me
This is the happiness I feel

# Once upon a time at Midnight...

Once upon a time at Midnight.... I am a Moonchild. Sometimes when I am riding I enjoy my talks with the moon. The night my soul cried, I bared my soul to the moon.

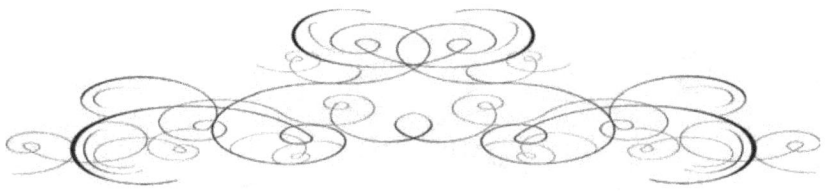

## Midnight

There is a moon in my window, it wanes
Faintly tilting its crown through fragile panes
Reach in my soul, and fondle my dreams
Massaging my dreams with luminous embrace
Rise and fall reckless across bare tracks
Wild soft assurance sway the universe
Rhythmic verses on an endless journey
An infinite journey, carved from undulating lips
Questioning why, why must you touch so deeply
Feel my rhythm capturing your season

*LaRedeaux*

# *Give me a night*

Moon so bright
Give me a night
To spend with you
Tell me everything is alright
Love me through and through
Moon so bold and bright
With you next to me
Don't deny me tonight
Oh Moon, sweet Moon

Give me a night
I'm hanging from a tree
For all the world to see
Give me a night
Brand me with your love
Give me a night
Under the stars above
Give me just one night

So you may see
That I want you always
Next to me
Give me a night
That never ends
Give me a night
That transcends
Give me a night
Purity of a white dove
Give me a night
Show me the true meaning of love

*LaRedeaux*

## *Get down tonight*

I make mistakes
I learn from them.
I am human after all.
This is my nature.
So please by all means
Take a little risk
Get down tonight.
Get down tonight.

## Full Moon

I asked the
Moon...
Do you love me?
Moon had nothing to say
I adore stars
But my heart...oh moon you hold
'O moon I fancy you'
Still the moon had nothing to say
Just shining brightly
Lighting my way
Until the clouds stole my moon away

# Ghetto Moon

The ghetto got its own moon,
Its own temptation,
Its own set of rules,
The ghetto got its own moon
Pregnant at midnight
The ghetto got its own moon
Hiding drugs that attack,
The ghetto got its own moon
Seeing all the blood, guns shed
The ghetto got its own moon
Watching his whore give head
The ghetto got its own moon
When the sun rose,
She was dead…

# Black

*B*lack has so many meanings...but for me BLACK *is* BEAUTIFUL. The night my soul cried, I released my thoughts on things BLACK.

*LaRedeaux*

## Black Love

Your black love I never want to leave
Your black love got me calling on the hour
Your black love gives me power
Your black love makes my heart sway
Your black love nourished me today
Your black love feels real deep,
dark love rooted in the night
Your black love will never take flight
Your black love is abundant the soul of me
Your black love conjoined but two
Your black love makes me sick, leaving me blue
Your black love allowed me to feel
Your black love I never knew could be real
Your black love
Your black love
Your black love sweeter than the juice
Your black love I couldn't turn loose
To your black love I cleave
Your black love will never leave.

# Black

**BLACK**

**BLACK**

**BLACK**

**BLACK**

**BLACK**

**BLACK**

BLACK is all I fucking see!
BLACK is all I'll ever be!
BLACK is the skin embracing me!
BLACK is the only thing you see…

*LaRedeaux*

## *Black Girl*

Black girl so filled with strife
                          Black…Black girl she'll take your life
Black girl free and wild
                          Black, Black girl, hate stole her smile
Black girl she shows no fear
                          Black, Black girl praise she cannot hear
Black girl won't see her cry
                          Black, Black girl just wants to die
Black girl hidden in the dark
                          You can't see her painful marks
Black, Black girl emerge like snow
                          Now Black/White girl shuck and jive…
You're now the Puppet's whore…

## My Sistah

My Sistah dry your eyes...

                                       My Sistah please dont cry

My Sistah don't end your life...

                                       My Sistah you're not his wife

My Sistah he's cold as a snake...

                                       My Sistah he's just a fake

My Sistah everything will be okay...

                                       My Sistah don't compromise your sway

My Sistah he's full of lies...

                                       My Sistah don't even try

My Sistah you're the one shining bright...

                                       My Sistah don't start a fight

My Sistah it ends tonight...

                                       My Sistah I need you, don't destroy your life

# My Brutha, Young Brutha

Can you see the mountain top?

Still in the valley, keep trudging, don't stop

My young Brutha, stop wasting your time

My Brutha, there's more to life than chasing dimes…

Young Brutha

My Brutha

Exceed the physical evaluation,

You're standing on the backs of men;

who changed the nation,

Young Brutha

My Brutha

Unfurl your brow

Change the pace, the time is NOW

Young Brutha

My Brutha

These words I share

I Love You, Believe a Sistah does care

My Brutha

Young Brutha!

## Black Gold

They flinch at my chocolate flavor,
In between the sheets I'm a fantasy
Desiring to take me to the brinks of ecstasy
Yet you loathe me in daylight...
Shun my color, clench your fist, so uptight
My colors shine bold, even when tarnished
You long to be hold
The sweetness emanating from the sacred wells
Your opaque elasticity, wagging tongues tells
My African posterior as curvy as a mountain outline.
Hips sway hypnotizing and sublime,
Dark and lovely I am an African queen
Only the like can be my King

*LaRedeaux*

# Woman

        She is a woman,
Strong woman,
        Grown woman,
Don't give a Damn
        She is a hurt woman
Damaged woman
        Unscrupulous woman
Beautiful rare Virtuous woman,
        A loving woman,
God-fearing woman,
        Trampled by many she still a woman
Open-minded woman,
        Waiting on Love woman
Adore that woman,
        Irreplaceable woman
Hear that woman,
        Don't fear woman,
There will never be another like that woman,
        She can change your life woman.
Revere that woman,
        Bitch doesn't know woman,
Be the MAN for that WOMAN!
        No replacing the *Black woman!*

## My Black Heart

You got me in love with a twist
Bringing my death quick with a kiss
You command my happiness to a halt
It's broken, but it's not your fault

Don't be sorry for the lies
I'm done with your cries.
My black Heart shakes
Feel the rector scale break

Shattered in many pieces
I am living in hell.
My black heart love doesn't dwell

I demand you leave, No I didn't ask
Perpetuating love behind the mask

Please stop...
No don't do that
Give that back…

## My Black Heart

How can you repair a heart that's Black?
Remove the layers
Tear them apart
Till nothing is left
But the faint drum

Desiring a spark
With my last breath
I breathe new life

Your Black Heart expired
When I removed the knife.

# Black Soul

My art leaps from the blackness of my soul
Emerging into shape at the call of love
There is no light without dark, two parts: not whole.
Visualize the forms of things above

Find strength
Flowing into shape called love.
Beauty in silence, the void and nil
Grace more than fire can kill

Conceive the birth of will
Majestic heights to which I aspire
Already paved, with
Blood, life and power.

Freed from captivity
Imprisoned in my brain
The voices that simmer remain the same
My virtuosity lingers in the blackness of my soul:

>There is no light without dark, two parts:
>I am now whole

## The Night My Soul Cried

I cried from the emotion inside.

My voice drowning in tears

Pain held me dear.

I struggled to get free.

Fighting the fights within me.

Seeking the time when happiness reigned.

So I cried and cried

Vulnerable

weak

I cried...

Tears are pouring out of my eyes

So I cried and cried

down on my knees

Love finally gave me strength

## Thank you

Thank you for being what you were;
Thank you for the ear you lend;
Thank you for advice that was rare;
Thank you, for being a true friend
Thank you for keeping my secrets;
Thak you for from within;
Thank you for not judging my sin;
Thank you for letting me in.
Thank you for sitting a spell;
Thank you for talking utmost sense;
Thank you for believing the fiction I tell;
Thank you for reading and not jumping the fence.

The end!

# Move forward

When was the last time you released? Here's your chance. Use the space below to let your soul cry.

1. Define your pain.

_____

_____

_____

2. Express that pain.

_____

_____

_____

3. Try to stay in the present.

_____

_____

_____

4. Stop telling the story.

_____
_____
_____

5. Forgive yourself.

_____
_____
_____

6. Stop playing the blame/victim game.

_____
_____
_____

7. Don't let the pain become your identity.

_____
_____
_____

8. Reconnect with who you were before the pain.

9. Focus on things that bring you joy in the moment.

10. Share that joy with other people.

www.ingramcontent.com/pod-product-compliance
Lightning Source LLC
Chambersburg PA
CBHW031453040426
42444CB00007B/1077